BOLD KIDS

MW01702010

North Dakota

CHILDREN'S BOOK WITH INTRIGUING INFORMATIVE FACTS

NORTH
CAP

DAKOTA
TOL

The state has a high percentage of millionaires per capita, as well as the longest coastline in the world. Christmas is celebrated in North Dakota on December 25th and is celebrated by both Christians and non-Christians alike.

Children in this state are often the future leaders of our diverse nation, so it's important to know about the state's history and culture and how it's changing. It's also an interesting place to visit if you're visiting with children.

Thousands of years ago, North Dakota was populated by Native Americans. The Mandan, Dakota, and Yanktonai tribes were among the first white settlers. In the 1820s, fur trappers dominated the area and were eventually replaced by ranchers and wheat farmers.

In the year 1861, North Dakota became an independent state and divided into northern and southern portions. The railroads brought new settlers to the state during the 1700s and 1800s. It was the 39th state to be admitted to the union in the following year.

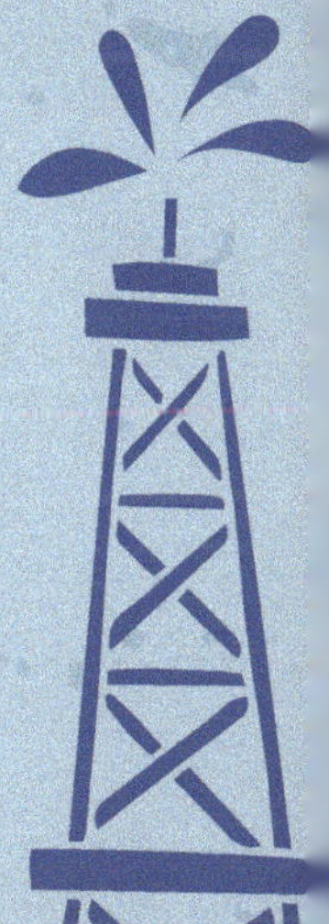

The state's name derives from the Sioux language, meaning friends or allies. French Canadians first explored the region in the 1738, after which it was acquired by the U.S. as part of the Louisiana Purchase.

A French-Canadian trader named Pierre Gaultier led an exploration party in 1738 to explore the Mandan territory. In 1812, Scottish and Irish families established the town of Pembina, which was part of the United States.

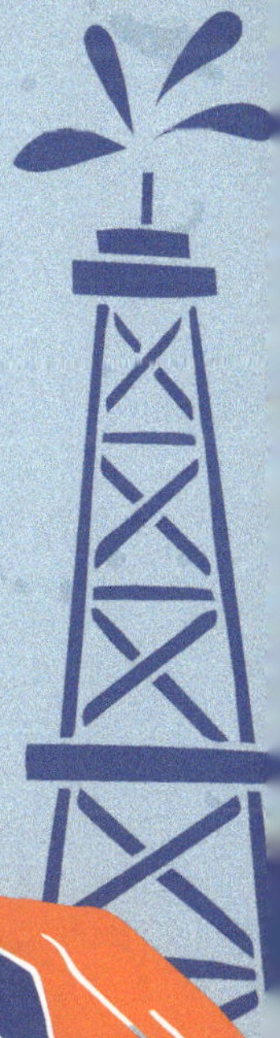

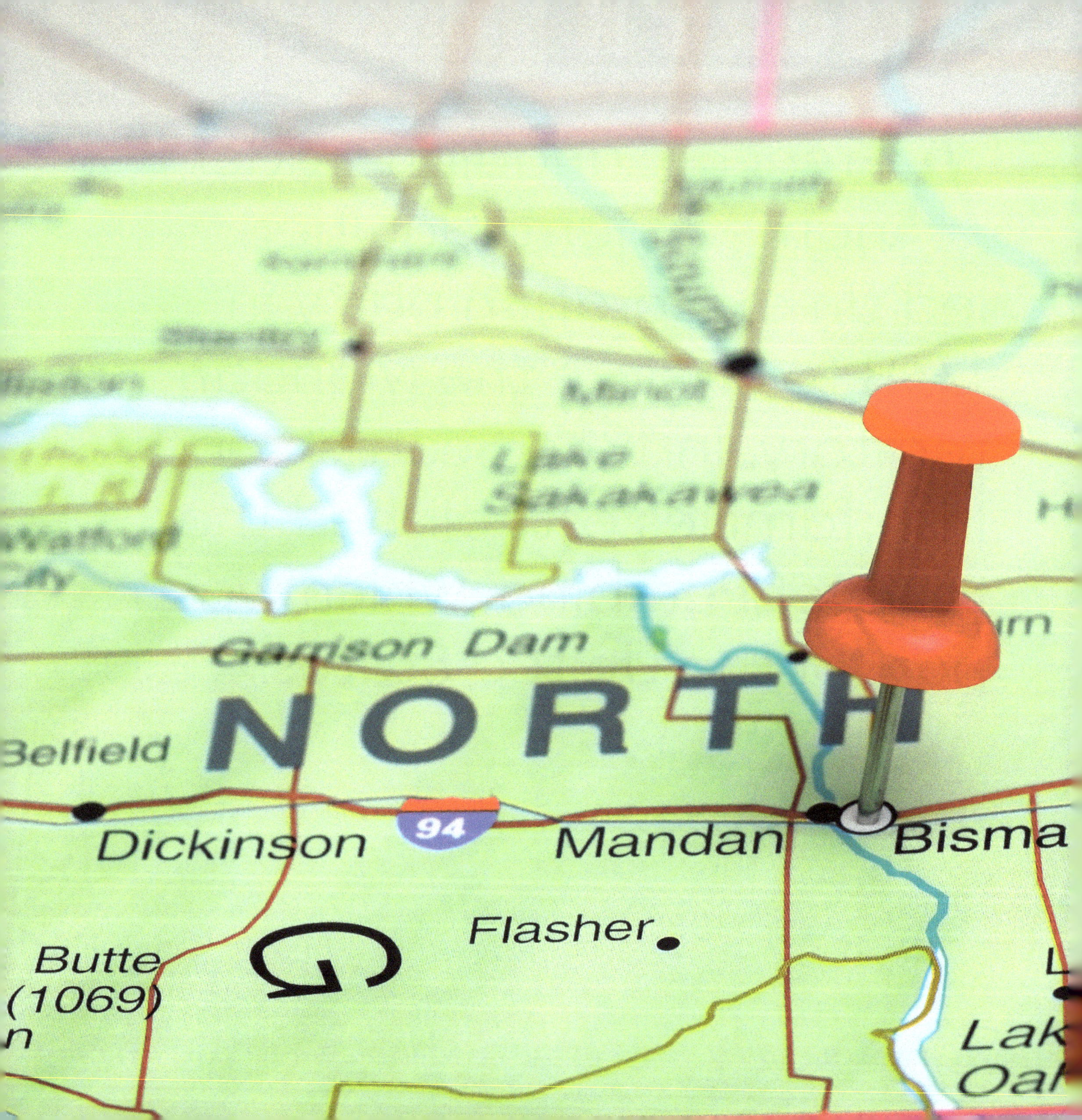
Garrison Dam
NORTH
Belfield
Dickinson
94
Mandan
Bisma
Flasher
Butte
(1069)

Sheyenne
Fort Totten
I. R.
Grand
Fork
New Rockford
AKOTA
Valley City
Jamestown
James
Lisbon
Ellendale

One of the most fascinating facts about North Dakota for kids is that the state has a continental climate. The state experiences hot summers and cold winters.

However, the climate of North Dakota is largely similar to that of most other states in the U.S. It is mostly a landlocked state, with an inland position. If you're visiting the state, you'll find a variety of interesting facts about it.

NORTH DAKOTA

Besides the state's diverse culture, North Dakota is home to the largest sunflower farms in the country. Its farmers produce enough wheat to make 12.6 billion loaves of bread, 113 million hamburgers, and 483 billion crayons a year.

The state's food production is a significant contributor to the world's food supply, and its rich heritage is a great source of pride for locals.

NORTH DAKOTA

This state is home to several Native American tribes. The Lakota and Dakota are the primary historic tribal nations in North Dakota. They call themselves the "Great Sioux Nation" and "Oceti Sakowin".

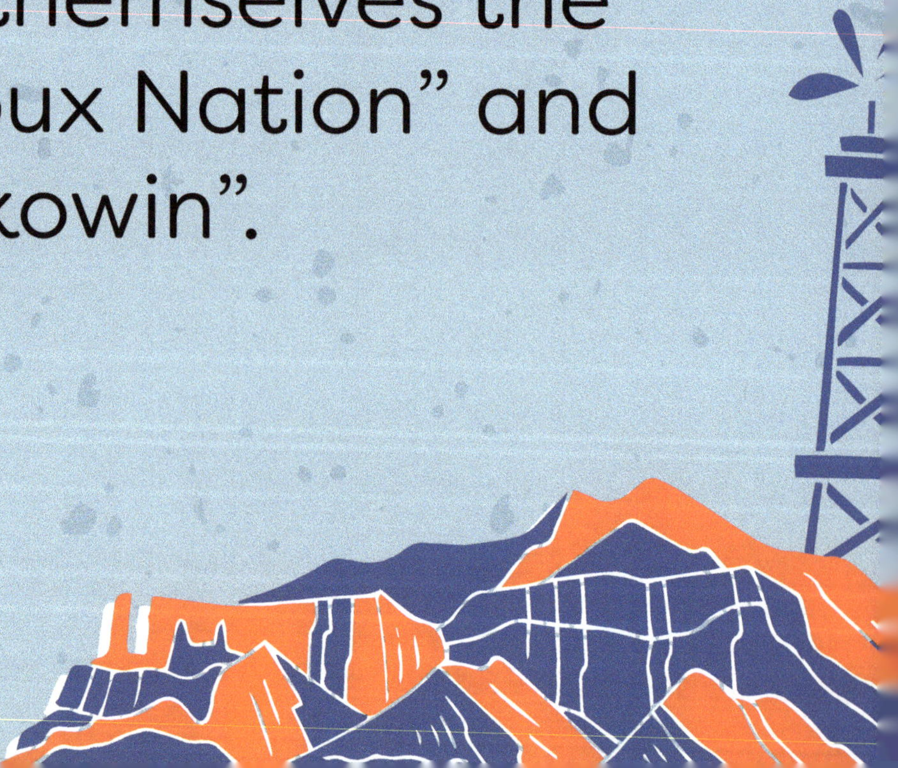

There are also the Blackfoot and Cheyenne, which are known as "Oceti Sakowin" in Canada. The last two tribes live in the region today, but the Lakota people lived in North Dakota for thousands of years before Europeans arrived.

In addition to being a major producer of sugarbeets, North Dakota is also a major producer of honey and lentils. During the winter, the state is also the second largest producer of potatoes.

Aside from producing these products, the state also has a variety of other products. Despite its small size, North Dakota is one of the most diverse states in the Midwest. The state is home to many industries, including the manufacturing of steel.

NORTH DAKOTA

The name Dakota comes from the Sioux language, which means "friendship." French Canadians first explored the area in 1738 and named it the "Peace Garden State". The names refer to the two countries' friendship and the beautiful landscapes.

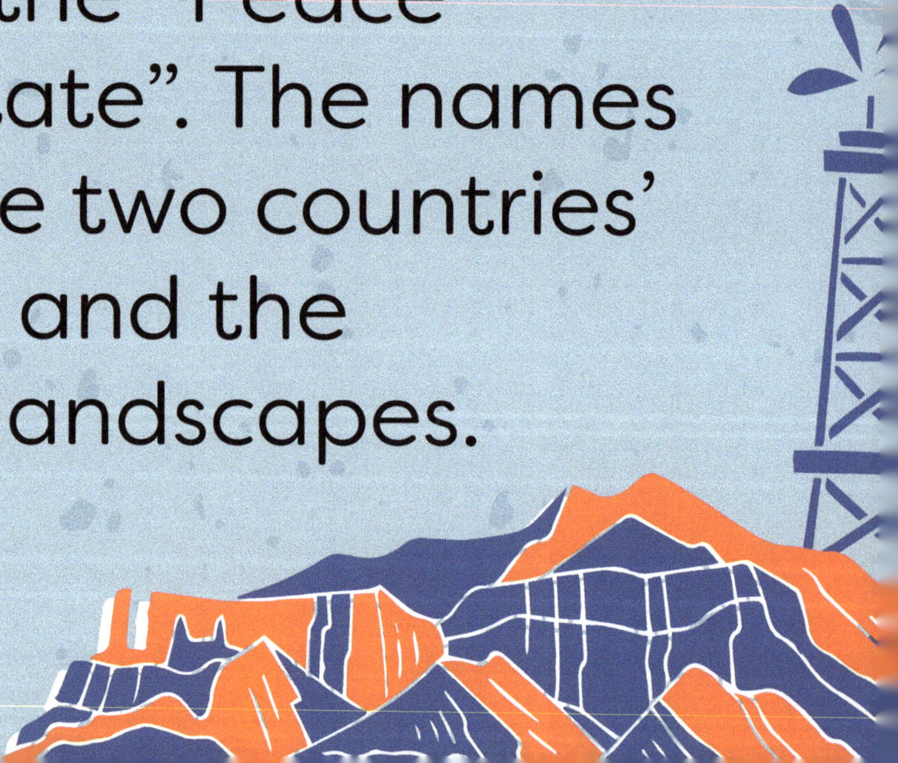

In addition to the state's beautiful nature, North Dakota is also home to the First U.S. Volunteer Calvary. In 1812, a group of Irish and Scottish families settled in the state.

Ingram Content Group UK Ltd.
Milton Keynes UK
UKHW052122310523
422672UK00007B/43

9 781071 710944